Shan-Tay Mercedes Watson

To whomever reads through these pages. I hope you are awakened and I hope you are healed and inspired

dmj publishing
& Web Design

[signature]

Facebook: Shan-Tay Mercedes Watson
IG: Shantay_mercedes.

DMJ Publishing & Web Design
www.dmjpublishing.com

Available from Amazon.com and other retail outlets

Live Performance Image (back cover) by:
Deezion™ IG: count_deezion

Cover Design by:
Donna M. Jacobs
info@dmjpublishing.com

First Printing, 2018

DEDICATION

To my daughter, you have been my only
constant, my motivation, my reason, my
heart flutter... my Bambi. Mom did her best
with what she had. I hope you are proud.
May you continue in perseverance, strength,
wisdom... AND JOY AND FUN !! (yolo)

ACKNOWLEDGEMENTS

To my readers, I appreciate the investment of your time to take this journey.

To everyone that has said one million times over the years "you need to write a book", thank you for the long pep talks about life, thank you for not accepting my fears, my procrastination or my excuses. Thank you for affirming that I have important stories to tell.

To Life... I've hated you and I've loved you. You don't make sense many times but you continue to teach me something new everyday and I am grateful to experience you. As we journey together, I embrace you with all that you have been, all that you are and all that is yet to come.

To DMJ Publishing, thank you for admiring and respecting my work and for caring about the purpose and vision and then bringing it to life.

INTRODUCTION

Yes, this is a book of poetry and if you are not into poetry, no worries as these writings are very blunt, understandable and candid. Each piece is vivid and follows a storyline. I urge you not to skip ahead.

In reading this book, you will travel along two roads of Audacity: one of the boldness, courage, fearlessness and bravery it takes for someone to face their challenges and to overcome them, the other aspect is that of life, people and circumstances seeming to be intrusive and sometimes plainly rude.

We find ourselves yelling "How dare this happen to me?" But after that, we must get to a place where we dig our heels in, pull out the grit, rise-up and be audacious.

These poems invite you to examine perspective, grace and compassion towards yourself and others as we all have a story. You will learn some of my path in these pages, but my hope is that you will find a message that impacts and inspires you.

Contents

x

THE PRICE

You don't get to know me
only on my polished days
as my treasure lies
in times where
I knew I was weakest.

These legs have
danced in thunderstorms
leaped over puddles
and did pirouettes
between rain drops

These struggles
are what beautified
the diamond
you may admire
which bears a heavy cost
to sing life's songs.

I will sing anyway.

UPROOTED

I used to be uneasy when people would ask me
where I was from
Simple question. Right? Not for an Over
thinker...
We have tendencies to make the simple
complicated... like
Do you mean where do I live now?
Or where I was born?
This was a loaded question for me
Because I hadn't yet decided where to claim
as HOME
Or better yet, WHERE claimed me

I've heard it said that it's not where you're
from,
But where you are.
Well, right now, where I am
Is not where I was born
Nor is it where I am from
Uprooted from one place to another and
Where I am now is my escape from that one.

I was born in the city of brownstones
Taxi cabs and trains and
Feet bustling past with no faces
Mommy and daddy, both were there Aunties,
uncles, grandparents, siblings, friends
Double-Dutch, Red Light Green Light and

Mother May I... on the top floor terrace
Tag through the hallways
Hide and seek through the streets and
dilapidated buildings

Fence climbing, rock throwing
Paper dolls and Barbie havens on the stoop
Boston baked beans, Chico sticks and Bon-Ton
potato chips
Pinatas, Birthday parties, Holiday parties
Crab parties and parties JUST to party

Rides in the back of the station wagon
Cousins crammed in between picnic baskets
Hikes and bikes and kites through central
park
Ferry rides to Bear Mountain and water slides

Of Twelve years I can't remember a time
of saying that I was bored or lonely
I had everything and everyone

And in the blink of an eye
And not for the sake of saying that saying
...but literally
I went to sleep one night in the place I was
born and
Awoke to black bags packed in the U-Haul

I went to sleep that next night in another state
The unfamiliar place where I must now say I
am from

No questions, no answers, no goodbyes.

This was the exile.

So, when one asks me where I am from.
My heart wants to say
I am from the city of brownstones,
Taxi cabs and busy trains
Feet bustling past with no faces

But that place is fading memories.

OUTCAST

New girl in town, reluctantly thrust amongst
the cliques
Already struggling with the life so abruptly
left behind
... Unfamiliar was the bed I slept in at night
No solace on the home front, no protection
from the outside

Already feeling out of place with my peers,
My pleas for mercy became overshadowed
Once I was targeted for ridicule and
persecution
There was no stopping the years of torment to
follow

I forgave them for the long walks home from
school
When I didn't know where the attack would
come from next
Looking over my shoulder, crossing to the
other side of the street
My heart violently thumping from my chest

I forgave them for the hockey stick nearly
killing me
When it was swung at my head with such ease
They thought not of the outcome if it
connected

Only that the blood thirsty crowd was pleased

I forgave them for the names they called me
For making others embarrassed to be around
Dating for me, was few and far between
Because I was the laughing stock of town

I forgave them for stealing the joys of proms
As large crowds began to paralyze me
What if they harass me or pulled a prank
Every day was filled with anxiety

I forgave them because a treasured moment
Was distorted, making me insecure
For me subconsciously disconnecting myself
To escape the embarrassment endured

I forgave them for making me call upon death
I swallowed sixty pills until I choked
Kept away for ten days and no one even
noticed
I became invisible, asleep inside, yet awoke

I forgave them understanding I had survived
for a reason
My strength was built to carry these stories
"Kids will be kids" is what they called it then
But BULLYING is what almost destroyed me

But I forgave them
Because they know not what they did

DEFLECTION (THE COVER UP)

So... you like to put others down to make
yourself feel better?
Well I wonder... how do you really feel?

Does your malice stem from wounds of years
past?
Were you made to feel inadequate? Were you
cast aside and dismissed?
Were you looked over and hung over... from
your overdose of tears?

I've come across your coldness many times
and I ve learned to take the high road BUT... I
have questions:

Is your attempt to crush others really a
wailing for help?
Is this a deflection from your misery seeking
company?

When your tongue lashes insults and when
your rage overtakes you
When you demean another, defame the name
of another, devalue another...
When you aim for the bull's eye and when you
think you have SCORED...
Do you feel better?

Do you feel accomplished having wounded

another...?
Inflicting the same injury that battered you,
leaving behind a legacy of your agony,
Trailing along in cowardice...carrying and
passing the poisonous venom
Seeping from your pores... lurking and craving
to infect others with negativity.

Too many people have given you a pass by
saying
"That's just how you are not to pay you any
mind"
...so, you've continued with your antics
Feeling elated by your two seconds of shine.

But I wonder....

How do you feel walking away from the waste
of your carnage?
When you are alone with yourself...
Do you FEEL better?...
Do you proudly look in the mirror or do you
recognize the sadness in your eyes?
...Silently questioning yourself...

Who damaged you and contaminated your
spirit?
What mutilated your heart and crippled your
hope?
Who impaired your compassion and numbed
your empathy?
What wreaked havoc on your soul?

I ask these questions because for SOME reason...

You feel the need to put others down to make yourself feel SOMETHING...
But... I truly wonder... Do YOU know how you really feel?

JAGGED LITTLE THRILL

I followed his eyes. He let me read the story
behind them.
I followed his smile. It filled the space in
any room.
I followed him into a field of excitement and
thrill.
His laughter had the power to heal my
world from hurting.
He was my **Remedy**.

I followed him into the freedom of myself
Loving vastly, wildly, living passionately
Forgetting the pressures momentarily as we
Drove through the city with our favorite
albums on our lips

I followed him into a world beyond my
understanding
Into HIS world thinking I could motivate
him OUT... but
I followed him instead, latching onto his
contagious energy

In our quiet times, I listened to his soul
speak
He said that his male bloodline rarely
survived twenty-four
I couldn't grasp that, couldn't fathom this

as reality
To me, all he had to do was get things
together, right?
Make some changes, right? Start fresh,
right?

He smiled THAT smile with a brave face to
put me at ease
Knowing I was treading in uncharted
territory
But I followed him his possibilities his
potential
I KNEW he started to see, started to
believe.
His hope began to burn bright

But ultimately, he was right. A jagged bullet
claimed his life
And stole his laughter as tubes aided his
last breath

I followed him... from a space once filled
with vibrancy
My will to love, my courage to feel...
Cleaved to his memory, seemingly following
him into death
Unable to reconcile the crossing of our
paths

The Lyrics replayed in my mind... "**Nothing
is Promised**"

Life was eclipsed by grief, forbidden to say
Goodbye
Struggled to forgive... No one to hear me
I was forced to keep my screams to myself
And within me, became my **Song Cry**.

Dammit Miz... **This Goes Out**

SEEKING SANCTUARY

Entered in with an open heart expecting to
release sorrows, not build fears
Never thought to be leery of the white collar or
thought he would prey on her tears

Skilled at misleading the wounded, encouraging
them to feel it's a place to belong
Cosigning on hopes and promises that the Lord
would fix all that was wrong

What? What was WRONG with me?

With so many rules and jargon, I eventually
caught on to church way of life
Desperately striving for the unattainable just
trying to have SOMEthing go right

Follow the leaders is what they'd teach, enable
blessings to the next level
"This was the will of God", they'd preach,
warning to not be labeled a rebel

Assigned to help me in a time of need but this
man of the cloth had other ideas
This gave him opportunity to be around me
when no one else could hear

His sexual pursuit caught me off guard asking
to spank away my disobedience

I stood in disbelief of his blatant and lustful
attempts of coercion

He rationalized that his collar was for church,
but outside he wore the shirt of a man
Placing fault on me for damage control,
suggesting I seek God to understand

So that God could... FIX me

I learned that problems were normally swept
under the rug
And I was encouraged to sacrificially take the
blame

That this man's purpose in life was bigger than
mine
And we should be careful not to expose him or
damage his name

As if there wasn't enough contention already
surrounding me
My sense of safety IN the four walls became
skewed

Assaulting the vulnerable using power and trust
Is a manipulative tactic of abuse in church too.

SUBMERGED

Flailing around in my mind, I would go
Just who was I at that time, I didn't really
know
I had spent many years being lost
Raped, molested abused and victimized
The mirror had only shown my shell
But never the sorrow behind my eyes

Bullied, attacked, assaulted and demeaned
Abandoned, rejected... Inside I would scream
DOES ANYONE SEE ME?

Probing around in the world, I sought
What was to become of me now, besides
distraught?

Motherhood found me at the age of seventeen
During dysfunction and perceived broken
dreams
But at least now, I had a purpose
My daughter would be the best part of me

This is IT... This is ME... A nurturer... THIS is
who I was meant to be

To break the generational curses carried and
prepare her to soar
But it hit me like a ton of bricks that one day
she won't need me anymore

She wasn't here to fill my voids or needs
Abandonment and rejection still lingered
Inside... I would scream
WHAT ABOUT ME?

Spiraling around in my soul, I went
On a search for mere relevance

I thought Jesus was the answer and
Believed He interrupted my suicide
I couldn't write that off as emotional zeal
The experience literally opened my eyes
New Hope, New Thrill, New Breath,
Spirituality
For a while, this lifestyle had worked
But somehow the foundation became
convoluted
When I experienced the same things in church

Bullied, attacked, assaulted and demeaned
Mishandled and abused ... Inside I would
scream
DOES ANYONE SEE ME?

COMFORT ZONE

She did not always have her own bed

She has slept in a bed with family
She has slept on a plastic covered sofa
She has slept on a stranger's floor
She has slept on the top of a bunk
She has slept in her best friend's bed
She has slept in his bed
She has slept on the courtyard bench
She has slept in a car
She has slept in bed with her child
She has slept in a hotel bed
She has slept in a hallway
She has slept on a train station bench
She has slept in a damp basement
She has slept in a hospital waiting room
She has slept on a futon

She did not always have her own bed

So when friends offer their spare beds to her
after late nights out... She opts to take the
long drives home instead... longing for her
own bed

Her bed was her luxury

Her bed was her comfort zone.

NEEDING SPACE

Sometimes... All I need is space
Although your issues may liken to mine
We can never comprehend the effects of the
ordeal
Another person may face

We don't know the process it takes for another
We don't know the patterns of another's
thoughts
We don't know the true status of another's
heart
We don't know the lessons their road in life
has taught

NO I DON'T want to talk about it
Hell, I don't even want to think
I also don't want to pretend nothing is
happening
While the walls around me continue to shrink

I... Just... Want Space

Sometimes your words add pressure and
Your expectations may deepen my wounds
The way we cope... It's just different
You may have good intentions
But it may be too much too soon

I don't want to shift my focus

I need to face the intensity, being true to
myself
Not pretending for you that I'm feeling better
Let me nourish my mental and emotional
health

SPACE... PLEASE

Understand... it's not about you and
It's not even about what you want for me
When my heart is crashing against my
thoughts and
The pain is leaning on my strength... PLEASE
... Just LET ME BE

And... give me some ... space

In MY own time, I'll grieve and deal, de-clutter
and cleanse
So I can breathe easy and see my way through
I'll conquer this hardship like the hundreds
before
And for your understanding, I'll greatly
appreciate you

For giving me ... some space

BLACKOUTS

There were times I would try to reflect
Tried to recall the small things
Tried to recollect any joys from my journey
But along the way, there were blackouts
Huge pieces of my past were missing

There are still many stories within me
Too many for one person to have carried
Chronicles full of run-on sentences
With hastily placed semicolons and commas

I took pride in my ability to keep it moving
With my natural inclination to survive
To fight and to take flight past the difficulties
Evidently, I was also good at locking in the
pain
Subconsciously burying misfortunes so deep
That even the good memories blacked out

I face those pauses of blackness
Sometimes frustrated from the pieces of time
That may never be recovered

Maybe all things are not meant to be re-
captured
Maybe some things are better left behind
But sometimes I run into familiar parts of me
That I cannot seem to grasp

They beg to reconcile with my soul
Clicking on my follow button

I choose to decline the broken pieces
I choose to create new images

PROCESSING

Some viewed me as rough and guarded
not knowing what I've processed through
While life had the audacity to throw vicious
curves
I had the audacity to emerge from my cocoon

Like the butterfly

My perspective isn't always clear
and my responses are not always effective
If triggered by the tunnel vision of those that
either experienced my weaknesses
Or ran with the vivid imagery
through the stories I've shared.
By perceptions ... I became boxed
into a polarized visualization of brokenness

But there is beauty in the process

My vulnerability, my sensitivity is daily proof
That my heart still beats alive
Part of the walking wounded, maybe
But with a vessel FULL of breath
I'm in tune with my humanity and
Welcome the transformation... the emerging

Like the butterfly

Some say I'm rough and guarded because I

have
Learned to set boundaries
preventing infections from negativity and pity
I'm not bitter and I'm not angry,
but I AM aggressively
...working through my sh*t
And sometimes... it's UGLY

Constantly refining the inner walls of my soul
As I acknowledge the truth of EVERY part of
me
I am then, another step closer to becoming
whole

Processing in progress

SHAME

They warned me not to tell anyone but God
And in that moment, you were given a name
I didn't know much about you at the time
But you were quietly known as SHAME

You began to walk with me daily
And I fought with you constantly
I don't deserve this, I don't want this, I'd
scream
Yet you were persistent and relentless in your
pursuit
To become one with my identity

Not quite visible to anyone else,
To me, you d make your presence known
Tapping me on the shoulder, irking me and
reminding me
Of how close we had grown

Well, I had no choice with you Shame
I cooperated to avoid us being exposed
I was sworn to your secrecy, almost paranoid
Always wondering if anyone else knows

THEY told me not to tell anyone but God
As if no one else had encountered you
So, I dragged you though my days and wished
you away at night

Until finally giving in to your truth

And I HID behind you Shame

I thought you were my punishment
So I suffered in pain, silence and guilt.
I walked around with a smile on my face
Falsely protected by the wall you had built

I wasn't in denial, but I did my best to avoid
you
Some days I just existed and struggled to deal
How... did I not see you coming to overtake me
YOU were the reason these wounds took so
long to heal

Within time, I began to learn your ways as
Your creeping was nothing new under the sun
You tried to hold me hostage in my mind,
isolating me
And trying to convince me I'm the only one

You set out to destroy my esteem
But I've decided to use you as a lesson instead
You may be a part of my history Shame
But you're not Who I am... I am a survivor
Of the Ignorance that society spread

THEY said... not to tell anyone but God
Because They were afraid and didn't
understand
But I educated myself and encouraged myself

And set myself to change the course of your plan

So now, I battle you differently
I USE you to make me more aware, conscious and stronger
My sob story, my guilt, my shame, you shall be no longer

No longer shall I feel disgraced
No longer shall I ask WHY
No longer shall I lose sleep for you
No longer shall I think of you and cry
No longer shall I give you power
No longer shall I wear you on my sleeve
No longer shall I cower in defeat
...when others find out that you've known me

What I know is HIS grace has been sufficient
And HIS power is made perfect in my weakness
So, SHAME on YOU SHAME
For making me feel I had a dirty little secret

You're ONLY an occurrence in life
And everyone has met you Shame
But now that I know how to navigate your afflictions
I will no longer dignify you with a name

THEY told me ... not to tell anyone but God
As if your part of my story isn't true

But what I know, despite what they say
Is there is more to me than what you put me
through
So...Goodbye Shame!

COURAGE ROUSED

I viewed a video of a couple
who had been married for 80 years
She had lost the capacity of verbal language
But you could see the love she had for him
Glazing over in her eyes
Gleaming through her smile and
in the overjoyed pats of her hands on his

The only word she could repeatedly utter
with varying inflections was...
"Hello"
Her face beamed as if
she was meeting him for the first time
...every 15 seconds.

He sweetly dialogued with her
His spirit interpreting the sentences
Between her "hellos"
The measure of their unity
only they knew

I won't have eighty years with my *"him"*

Life cannot extend our days
To fulfill this length of time
Life cannot turn back to
Retrieve the hours I haven't known him

I can only dare to imagine

That when my "he" finally arrives
The quality of our love
Will vibe as deep as eighty years

CAPTIVATED

What do I do?
What do I say?
What are you doing here?
Whispering these loud thoughts
to myself because
You were right
where I needed you to be
The beating of my heart was racing
the rhythm of your breath

I tried to hold time still in that moment
Fighting off the fear of past heartache
For once, I was present

You were a sight for sore eyes
Your voice was ointment
A soothing balm in the right places
Your eyes were a cloud of comfort
I was hurt and then relieved
I was scared and then refreshed
It's been a very long time since
feeling wasn't so heavy.
with you, it was easy.

I was reminded that
I could embody
More than sadness
He reintroduced hope

BEWILDERED

I don't write many love poems because I don't
want to gift a painting to those who recklessly
vacated my space. If they were so hasty to
trash the home of my heart and ransack my
mind, why leave footprints back to me for
them to trace?

He was a "once in a blue moon" encounter,
that gave me hope and stimulated the
erogenous zones of my mental, digging deeper
into my truth than expected and easily sharing
more than we planned to

I displayed strength through my transparency,
being open, not making this "getting to know
you" process difficult, showing that I can
disarm my walls, communicate and trust,
without my history hindering expressions felt

What gets me is... All along

He knew my efforts would never be enough
for him, knew there was never intentions
to explore possibilities. Hindsight, I picture
him inwardly laughing the more I disclosed,
impressing himself with his persuading
abilities

Damn I felt so naive...

He said he never expected to mesh deeply
and it's best not to entertain me at this
time in his life. He thought his apology was
letting me down easy, but this "kindness" was
adulterated with excuses and lies

I won't put the full ownership on him and I
admit the slap in the face bruised when he
chose to leave. I obviously don't know how to
play this game and got caught with my heart
on my sleeve.

What's considerate is not to awaken a
woman's love before it's time, not to take the
road of cowardice, not to litter the beautiful
lake of my emotions having no aspirations of
ever loving me

I walked on nails of courage to get close to
him... and when I reached him, he offered no
band aide or gauze. This heart says that if it
must experience anymore bruises to write
bewildering poems, it would rather bow out of
scribing its falls.

I know how to face disappointments. I've been
through enough to know how to get up and
move along, but this one had me wondering
IF this "what if" could have been a place to
belong.

VULNERABLE REFLECTIONS

She reflects on nights like this...
...Just the slightest thought of the modest
swipe of his hand endearingly cuffing her
shoulder.

Have you ever felt such magnetism? A line
of energy flowed from the tips of his fingers,
penetrating her skin and spreading like a
wave beneath her surface.

Have you ever skipped a rock in the river and
watched the water reverberate outward?...
Well, yeah... like that!

The first time they kissed... laying side by side
staring at each other... through the blanket
of darkness that separated them... their
connection broke the shadows and spoke
in the silence as she beckoned him to pass
through. He answered with his lips finding
hers.

Not to be melodramatic, comparing this to
fireworks... but this was surely a work of fire...
A surge, a flare that momentarily disrupted
their anxieties,

Blazingly Sensual... yet, mesmerizing and
gentle ... Taking her to the very peak of

sexual... but instead...he wraps her in the cuff of his arm and kisses her forehead, bidding her sweet dreams. Leaving her tender and eager pressed against his chest for the remainder of the night.

She lay awake as the moonlight peeked until the sun dawned; Counting each breath he took, admiring his peaceful slumber, dreading the buzz of the alarm clock that was sure to startle him awake and whisk them into the frenzy of the day.

As she sensed a hindrance... the long and quiet days in between was foresight of the eventual end of their nights like this. She knew he wasn't there to stay. She knew his mind was too far away.

With her intuition tugging below, she conceded and tucked the blissful reflections away... Choosing to keep her memories of him sweet.

INTROSPECTION

I had placed a bed inside the corridors of my
heart and
I complacently laid there. It was peaceful.
The door was guarded by a sniper's rifle as its
latch.
The shades were drawn most times and
The insulation muted the noise.
Inside my fort, I didn't have to reason with
The disturbances of the world

Sometimes I would peek out of the window
And remember the turmoil
Sometimes I would listen at the door
And recall the loud cries
Sometimes I wondered if the seasons had
changed
But I would recount the deceptions of the
forecast

So, I kept shelter, kept busy
Rocking and humming and knitting together
The pieces of my past

One day, a presence appeared before me
Somehow, penetrating my walls without
triggering alarms
How did you know I was in here?
She gently answered... I AM YOU!

I felt the blood warmly pumping through my
bosom
Ice slowly beginning to melt
Tingles vibrating, shaking this space until
The numbness carefully released its grip

It was then that I realized that
"I" was the pain that was trapped beneath the
anger
The walls that I had built for my protection
Instead, locked me inside of my own darkness
I held myself hostage, letting the mail pile up
At the door as if... no one lived there.

My rescuer introduced herself as Destiny
And asked... are you ready to escape?

ESTEEMED

This morning I awoke and laid in bed
Enjoying the stillness in the air
Visualizing my day with great expectation
Knowing that

THIS... IS THE DAY

I had a decent night's sleep
The sun was peeking through the corners
Of my blackout curtain
Today, there would be no rain, no clouds
No... Not Today... because
This day... would be one of clarity and peace

THIS IS THE DAY

That my feet will stand firmly on the floor
That I will love what I see
Instead of the days I would face the mirror
Disappointed because I didn't recognize
The beauty in my reflection

Surely, the mirror must have been defective
The features, the silhouette was deceiving
I saw... a shell incompletely sculpted
Through MY eyes of contempt

BUT

THIS... IS THE DAY

That I am completely in synch
I looked at every part, every inch of me
And I very much enjoyed the sight

Good Morning Beautiful

WORTHY

You'll have to say it when
the circumstances don't show and prove
You'll have to pull and tug on your faith
when your feet can't seem to move

You'll have to look in the mirror...No...
Not at your outer reflection
But through the gateway to your soul
You'll have to gaze hard at that inner child
who is struggling to become whole

... and tell yourself

I AM WORTHY

You'll have to stare in the face of your fears
That kept you bound for so long
You'll have to silence that voice
That told you, you don't belong

You'll have to muster up the strength
When you feel unable to speak
Every day you'll have to tell yourself
While you're dusting off defeat

I AM WORTHY

You WILL see adversity strike
And the battle will seem lost

You'll have to war on your own behalf
And be ready to pay the cost

You'll have to kick and scream
At the things you cannot understand
You'll have to believe that in all things
There's a bigger plan... because...

YOU ARE WORTHY

Your family may no longer push you... and
Your friends may no longer lead the cheer
Your spouse may no longer have soothing words
Your employer may no longer need you there
You may have prayed for that relationship
You may even feel you have been cursed
You may feel lonely, tired, unloved, unheard
You may begin to doubt your worth... but... NO

YOU ARE WORTHY

You'll have to let what's dead
be buried and gone
You'll have to let whoever left your side...
Mosey right on along

You'll have to embrace those who reciprocate
And are going in the same direction
You'll have to fall down time after time after
time...
While embracing your imperfections

You'll have to be active in your journey

Even if the path is looking disgraced
You'll have to remember the times
You went through fire and water
And was brought out to a wealthy place...
because

YOU ARE WORTHY

Yes, we are to walk lowly, in meekness, long-
suffering
And the love of others to forbear
BUT we are also to walk worthy of what's
within us
Assurance carries us to that place called
THERE

WE ARE WORTHY

BEAUTIFULLY IMPERFECT

It s time I pledged Kindness to myself...
Because Me has been forgotten amongst the
rubble in my mind
Striving for perfection because I
didn't want to get it wrong... Again
Didn't want to lose... Again
Be blamed... Again
Fall... Again
Miss the mark... Again
Be alone... Again
Disappoint... Again
Be misunderstood... Again
Judged... Again
Be strung along... Again
I didn't want to have to explain Again

Explain Why... I wore make-up on my
blemishes

In panicked attempts to correct and perfect
I would plan EVERYTHING
Plan One, Plan Two, Plan Three
And even backed those up with Plans A, B & C

Liberty wasn't in my comfort zone because...
I always needed to know what was next
As authentic as I knew my heart was
My actions were contrary

Most times, even leaving myself perplexed

I was stagnant in rumination... Over-thinking
How can I make my life go RIGHT?
How can I illuminate the good things only?
How long until the struggles come into sight?

How long... can I keep the make-up on my
blemishes?

What happens if I can't control the outcome?
What happens when the plan is intercepted?
I had to face it that life does not work like that
Climbing a never-ending ladder to "I have it
All figured out blvd"
... only to come crashing down flat?
I'm pledging kindness to myself because
I never gave the real me a real chance
People pleasing became easy
Pushing you further than I pushed me
Hiding in the background shrinking what I had
achieved
While others saw this as false humility

Because the make-up was the perfect shade
for my blemishes

I subconsciously dumbed myself down
To fit into the accepted
Which I never could accept
or respect because
Underneath the layers

I knew there was something
EXCEPTIONAL
about me

Born to make waves
Unique in all my ways and
I had to pull this truth to the surface
And give myself... Grace

So, I'm removing the make-up from my
blemishes and
Walking on the cobblestone road of

"I AM GOOD ENOUGH"

It's alright to make mistakes AND go on to be
great
It's fine not to know the ending AND to simply
have faith
It's alright to get it wrong AND to want to get
it right
It's fine to lose some battles AND be proud to
have fought the good fight

It's ok to say yes AND no or to wing it and just
let life be
It's Good Enough to be Beautifully Imperfect
The make-up is OFF my blemishes
It's time that I honor kindness to ME

AUDACIOUS

She Speaks... with intention
She Speaks for NOW & tomorrow
She Speaks with SOUND, clarity and
conviction
She Speaks from her joys and her sorrows

She was mocked for her words of eloquence
and passion
By the shallow, she was deemed too deep, too
intense
Her inflections roar from the depths of her
being
Because she remembers those times WHEN...
... she felt she shouldn't speak

As if broad vocabulary is a bad thing or a
"white" thing
Her peers had need to correct her, suggesting
"cooler" words to use
The criticism once stifled her tongue and
Eventually silence was the way she would
choose

She remembers the pathway where her voice
was lost
The passageways through which her words
were stripped
She remembers the times she was warned...

NOT to tell
Learning early on to seal harmful secrets on
her lips

She recalls the times her appeals went
unheard
And the times her views were not considered
She recalls her wisdom being discounted in
youth
And the backlash causing her voice to wither

She SPEAKS UP now because others have
tried to tell her story
She SPEAKS UP now not being passive or
aloof
She SPEAKS UP now refusing to take on
misconceptions
She SPEAKS UP in protection of her truth.

She SPEAKS UP for the voiceless
She SPEAKS UP lighting the lane of
possibilities
She SPEAKS UP to showing scars and
triumphs
She SPEAKS UP to represent Victory

About the Author...

Shan-Tay Mercedes Watson was born in Brooklyn, NY, raised in Norristown, PA and has one magnificent daughter.

Shan-Tay has lived and breathed artistry all of her life and was a natural dancer. She used this gift of dance to perform inspirational messages for 13 years. She is a lover of words and began writing poetry in her youth and was later introduced to Spoken Word performance.

Shan-Tay saw both passions as not only an avenue for coping, healing and expressing herself, but also as an opportunity to be an example and a vehicle of inspiration for others. She transparently shares her personal life experiences to expose the reality, effects and victories over adversity and trauma, encouraging others to overcome.

From these passions, Shan-Tay became a Certified Crisis Counselor, formerly working as a victim advocate, providing intervention and support services for sexual assault victims, other serious crime victims, bullying and suicide prevention.

For more information or booking requests:
Email: smwatson8@gmail.com
IG: shantay_mercedes

AUDACITY

If you heard your story or could relate to any of mine, please write a review on www.amazon.com to encourage me and others. We would love to hear from you.